A LITTLE SALVATION

The University of Georgia Press
Athens and London

JUDSON MITCHAM

A Little Salvation

POEMS OLD AND NEW

A BROWN THRASHER
BOOKS ORIGINAL

Published by The University of Georgia Press
Athens, Georgia 30602
© 2007 by Judson Mitcham
All rights reserved
Designed by Mindy Basinger Hill
Set in 10.5/14 Adobe Jenson Pro
Printed and bound by Maple-Vail
The paper in this book meets the guidelines for
permanence and durability of the Committee on
Production Guidelines for Book Longevity of the
Council on Library Resources.

Printed in the United States of America

11   10   09   08   07   P   5   4   3   2   1

Library of Congress Cataloging-in-Publication Data
Mitcham, Judson.
A little salvation : poems old and new / Judson Mitcham.
      p.   cm.
"A Brown Thrasher Books original."
ISBN-13: 978-0-8203-3038-9 (pbk. : alk. paper)
ISBN-10: 0-8203-3038-8 (pbk. : alk. paper)
I. Title.
PS3563.I7356L58 2007
811'.54—dc22   2007015085

British Library Cataloging-in-Publication Data available

The publication of this book was made possible in part by generous gifts from Rosie Kay and Lane Stewart.

FOR JEAN, ZACH, AND ANNA

Contents

T W O. From *Somewhere in Ecclesiastes*

THREE. From *This April Day*

Acknowledgments

Poems in this volume have been selected from *Somewhere in Ecclesiastes* (Missouri, 1991) and *This April Day* (Anhinga, 2003).

Some of these poems, or versions of them, appeared in *America, Antioch Review, Black Warrior Review, Chattahoochee Review, Devil's Millhopper, Georgia Review, Gettysburg Review, Habersham Review, New England Review, Poetry Miscellany, Poetry Northwest, Prairie Schooner, River Styx, Snake Nation Review, Southern Poetry Review, Southern Review,* and *Tendril.*

"The Foolishness of God Is Wiser Than Men" was published in *Poetry.*

"Preface to an Omnibus Review" was reprinted in *Harper's.*

"Explanations" was reprinted in *The Pushcart Prize XIV: Best of the Small Presses,* 1989.

"Promise" and "Tennessee" were published in the *Georgia Review* (Summer 2007).

A LITTLE SALVATION

ONE. New Poems: Oblique Lexicon

Art

Questions for the mockingbird: why call back
to the cricket and cicada?

You should always be at work, don't you think?
Fooling some female or controlling the yard,

mocking the kingbird or the nightjar,
not a cat's moan, not the whine of a screen door.

And why catch that blues note from the radio
so exactly? It disappears

with the passing car, and you are there to hold it,
but why? How cruel you are.

2

Those sheds buried under kudzu are too easy.
The wine-hued roofs over ruins of barns,

the rotted-out houses—where's the news?
So there's no aroma of fried okra,

no box of air where the kitchen was.
A chimney remains—how many have you seen?

Say again what the weeds mean. Maybe
they exist for the story itself, to let us know

how late the day grows,
but who's confused about that? Is it not

time for some brighter pain? Make it a road,
I say, and make it wide. Lay twelve lanes

over the homestead. Let there be a wild
river of traffic here, a different oblivion.

Go on.

Body

Let no one explain
the parable of the hot dog gobbled at the ball game.

Let no one illuminate

any quick turn through eternity it might take,
any odd bit of the kingdom it might assume.

The rat hair and roach wing
we have swallowed—whose sacraments are these,
whose secrets?

How guilty the body is. Some days,
the simplest things matter,
and you are fascinated by water, there at the faucet,

watching it flash and break, amazed at being alive,
washing your face.

2

Not shaped like an apple or pear
or anything that would go soft and rot; not like any
accoutrement of sport—Titleist or tennis ball—

this knot of cells, calcified, building itself
for years, like a thoughtless practical joke—
outrageous, with no one to witness it—

5

in the cerebellum. It resembled,
more than the usual edibles or things of play,
an act of weather, a giant chunk of hail. Hard,

like old ice, they told us, after drilling it out.
Our mother had a twitch in her eye, nothing more,
when I took her to the doctor,

eleven years ago, this September.

Close

Alone, sick on Christmas,
I drink Scotch and watch the folks across the road.
Around noon, they walk out

past the carport and arrange themselves
at their leisure. Three women relax
at the trunk of someone's black Saturn. Four men

walk off by themselves,
a good ninety feet up the drive. One of the women
sits on the back of the car;

another sways, as if to music, and sweeps a foot
at a pinecone. Two girls,
maybe four and seven, kick a ball around

in the front yard. Then, oddly,
as if bound to a bad script, they go in, one by one,
and they're gone,

only the empty yard and the lonely car
in my binoculars.

Clown

But why can't a clown get some downtime?
I'm always on. (Even though

I don't use the goofy nose or the long shoes,
I do admire

a certain polka dot jumpsuit.) Why does a fool
get no furloughs? *Whose*

show must go on? The only solo,
bozo, is your own. So go ahead, tell the joke.

It's no big deal. But listen, jokerhole,
make it a real joke.

Don't fake another fall. *Did you hear the one
about the professor who left his soul*

*to the medical school, and his body
to the First Baptist Church? Is this thing on?*

Dead

You are dancing in your car, caught

slipping into the deep bass of "Exodus," the spirit-
voice of Bob Marley,
letting your shoulders go with it. You would laugh,

too, if you saw yourself, and if
you were someone else, because
there is a blindness in us all, and here it is:

you are ridiculous to the folks suddenly
beside you in their car
and who can't hear the song. It says *open your eyes*,

it says *are you satisfied*
with the life you're living? If you can't dance,
alone in your car,

to Bob Marley, you may be dead already.

2

At the old Y downtown, the framed photos
along the halls show boys' teams
from the teen years of the last century—

all white boys, posed around
a basketball with a raised seam. I see them
pendulum free throws

from between their knees. I see them
sling those two-handed sets from way out.
The team's dead now,

but each player has a name, still,
that weighs what yours does, or mine,
exactly, and always will. Look how

those dead boys have slicked back their hair.

Directive

Drive out after the rain, late in July,
late in the day, along the two-lane

where the grape smell of the alien vine in flower
sugars the air, where the kudzu not only

embraces the land but the bull pines and the white oaks,
grows along limbs and down through tire swings,

hides the old outbuildings, negotiates
the locked gates and the barbed wire, and holds fast.

Follow that road
maybe five miles and turn right, you'll hit the interstate.

Note that it has no excitement over you;
that the man running the Circle K greets you

too politely, you think, in his throaty Punjabi.
Buy your bottle of water. Take a drink.

Dream

1

A bad night of no sleep at all, and then
you recall a dream, realize you've dozed,

but you don't know when. The word *dream*,
made of mead-buzz and music

and whatever the scop brought to the party,
first meant joy, merriment, noise.

That sense of the word died out
about a thousand years back, and the other—

vision or deceit or ghost—took over,
and it's ours. How tricky, just to sleep,

but to dream what you need, get back there
to that lost joy, how rare.

2

Jump salty at the wrong time, Jimmy did.
Ends up sad as God, not in jail, not yet.
What could the woman want?
Not you, old buddy, & nothing you can get.
Let the truth come on out now, Mr. Man.
Nobody in your bed.

Verily, verily, I say unto you,
Jimbo, anything I damn well want to.
Who's that wearing blackface?
All right, then. Think he too smart to die.
Mutter spiffy, if it gets too heavy.
Me? I'm talking to you,

whose name is not Jimmy & whose ideas
ever were not these. Easy for you to say.
Days race by without love.
That woman, Jimmy, she have her own life.
There ought to be a law against those eyes.
—Mr. Man: There is.

3

My brother and I heard the rumor:
he was out there alive.
So we drove to the grave, shoveled crazily,
and wrestled our father out of the box.
God be praised.
Eight years earlier, we'd made a mistake.
Today, just in case,
we'd brought along the old kitchen table
and a Sunday meal—beef, rolls and gravy,
our mother's chocolate cake.
He raised both hands to his beard,
as if surprised. Stupidly,
I asked him how he'd been,
and his eyes resurrected a flatness
that we recognized,
and he answered me with one word, *dead*,
his timing still deft and his voice
easy with the obvious. The three of us
laughed like fools. I awoke
with his bony hands grabbing for the rolls.

Epilogue

Yet why not say what happened? Is it because,
even now, in the quick of the day, looking here
and looking there—so alert

you can't stay in one place, can't remain where you are—
you are dreaming away your life, floating off
into some old El Dorado of nowhere?

Is it because those photos in the box, mixed
and shuffled, little rectangles and squares
of forever, are full of strangers,

and you are one of them? Because
the ball of ice cream balanced on the sugar cone
in the snapshot is not still cold, not still

holding that shape, not still raised and on its way
to the boy's mouth, open comically as it waits
for the lost taste? Is it because, somehow,

you cannot give him—not even him—his living name?

Etiquette

June goes gaudy with bad boutonnieres—
flamingo mimosas, the giant
magnolia's bowl of petals. Let us consider

the man not welcome at the wedding.
What's the etiquette for the bad father?
What's the right flower for the ignored-

with-good-reason, the uninvited? A hydrangea,
head wide as a cabbage; or the bull thistle
wild along the roads; or a dandelion,

only a stalk stuck to his lapel by the time
he insists on their dance? He is a sad weed
himself, this man who has no daughter

but tries to hold her.

Forever

1

I will never forget Clive Wearing and his wife,
Deborah. Every term,
for a decade, teaching Intro Psychology,
I showed the same video: a virus
had destroyed his hippocampus.
He came home one day with a headache
that would not quit. Three days later,
he was shipwrecked in the past—
that day he came home—
and the right now. Whenever
Deborah opened his door, having left him
only seconds before, Clive leapt to his feet.
He hadn't seen her in years.
He'd swing her in his arms. He would sing.
In line after line of his diary, he wrote,
"Awake for the first time now" and "I adore
Deborah forever."

2

Who will give us tomorrow forever?
There's a moon in the window, forever.

What's the long night for, and who will tell us?
There is no way to ask, though, forever.

Will you think of me, lost in the old house?
How can I miss you so, and forever?

Will you wake in the night, without sadness?
There is nowhere to go now, forever.

And whoever I am, here's my answer.
In our small boat, we'll row out forever.

Gift

He lies back on his bed,
lets the globe rest lightly in his right hand,

guides it with his left. Over and over, he lofts it
as close to the ceiling as he can.

What he's trying for
is to flip that facsimile into the air so precisely

that the slightly raised places—
the Appalachians, say, or the Pyrenees—graze

the skin of paint, make the earth pause
where it is, with a

faint scrape, a baby gasp, and drop without spin,
dead-fall, into his hands.

All the rainy afternoon,
this is what he does, till his brother wanders in,

looks around and bends over,
for all the world, a perfect target. What brother

will not pelt him, happily,
with the planet, that gift they have to share?

So it puts a little dent in the globe.
Nobody asked for it.

Grace

This is a letter to Miss O'Connor.

Haven't I seen you on a concourse in Atlanta?
Is that your heaven? Are you not
at the gate, looking hard, trying to get the point

of the tattoo too blue to read, the keloid scar,
the sad red bubble of hair? Do you watch her
forever, that girl whose lips move,

who gives herself a headshake, who reassures
and comforts her one small bag, strokes it
with her good hand? Haven't I seen you,

clear eyed, watching the haze
beyond the last gate, as if Jesus were coming in
on the nine o'clock from Charlotte?

Aren't you holding a ticket?

2

Flannery, at eight, fights the angel
who's always beside her. How she hates that.

She whirls, sudden as Christ,
throws an elbow to his throat, an uppercut

to his lungs. She lunges at the air
where he is, easy prizefighter of grace

who feints and slides away. Maybe he smiles.
Let him smile.

She will have her blessing. She will be,
for eternity, a throbbing in his wing.

3

Yesterday, at Jim's funeral,
a moment of grace,

when a baby held by a man
standing along the wall

began to draw in its tiny breath,
midelegy, with the first

clicks of the hiccups. People
turned, as if for comfort,

toward the little noise. *Christ
will come like that.*

History

Negroes for Sale:

Woman and 2 children,
8 and 3,

together or separately,

sold for cash
or traded for groceries.

Several small boys
without their mothers.

Hymn

using lines from *Jubilate Agno*

Let the tongue untie itself.
Let the beatitudes do what they do.

For there he heard certain words
which it was not possible for him to understand.

Let the dust rise and walk. On his last day, let the old man
lay down a bet.

For there is a mystery in numbers.

Let the fool do his little dance.
Let the lonely go sleepwalking out of the house.

For there is a language of flowers.

Let the liar not look at the moon.
Let the graveyards guard each beloved from rude apocalypse.

For infinite upon infinite they make a chain.

Let the blue sky of evening ease us down.
Let the glory be a surprise. I have my prayers.

For they are together in the spirit every night
like man and wife.

Idiom

To dance in Bethlehem. To cry thumb. To take
the moon with your teeth. To see nothing but blue.

To throw the house out the window.
To curve your back. To have liver. To be an oil.

The joy is in the well.
Another pair of sleeves. To lead the dog

through the barnyard. To unveil little altars. On
the other song. To drop your arms. Under under.

Around around. To see thirty-six candles.
A blue story. Black work. A green old man.

A man of three letters. An ass at the lyre.

Ignorance

God, where could a man begin?
Where, big man? Let's educate the dead.
What do the white man know?
Look here, Mr. Jim: hold out your right hand.
Ever hear yourself talking & does not
realize who it is?

Jimmy & his boys played loud in graveyards.
Didn't know no better, did they now?
Got tore down & they played.
But who needs to know? Would that be you,
Casper? Slip me the money. Do it now.
You *do* know who I am?

Well, Jimmy have a problem. He do:
why he talking this way? Mainly because
he needs to. Don't you know
he did not much like the Negroes? But God,
listen how they talk. All right, Mr. Man.
Go on. Listen.

Jubilate

Inside the human body, the larvae mature and grow as long as three
feet. After one year, the threadlike worm emerges slowly through a
painful blister in the skin. It is pulled out a few centimeters each day
and wrapped around a small stick, a process that can take months.

For I will consider the guinea worm.
For he is nowhere, a spirit in the water.
For he slips in, a mystery, a cool drink, an echo of thanks.
For he is silent forever, even broken in half, even snapped off as he is
  drawn out.
For he is slow.
For he is slow to make himself known.
For he is the servant of the Living God, duly and daily serving him.
For he shakes and trembles with laughter, but he never laughs.
For he opens the throat wide to old prayer, raw sound without a
  name.
For he breaks out hot, a needle from the fire, blister water from the
  pond.
For he is never mistaken, but he is not vain; he is a sliver of praise.
For he gathers himself in many arms.
For he humbles the young and the old, easily; he sends them home.
For the nations come after him.
For he flashes and squirms, something else, through the dreams of
  his absence.
For he waits there, underneath the gold sun floating on the pond.
For he forms his one nest under the skin, curled in on his whiteness.
For he is good to eat breaded and fried, a fatty treat for the mad.
For he holds on, and he holds on, as if he cannot forget.
For he is good to think on, if a man would express himself neatly.
For he is simple, the number one, but hard to count.
For he measures each eye that will watch his coming out,
  each eye that will not.   25

For he goes in innocent, he knows no deceit, and he will hold
nothing back.

For he is one thing first, unseen in the water, and then he is another.

For he is crushed underfoot.

For he comes unaware into his one shape, unable to stop.

June

Call it anything you want.
Call it Orange Coal of Hope, call it False Pearl.

The daylily, all June, turns loose
blossoms on the day,

lets the beauty do its work. Late in June,
when the day makes strange wine out of rain,

call it The Last Blue Flame of the Afternoon.
Call it The Firewheel of Summer.

Every June day is always a Sunday.
Every Sunday, for me, a day in June.

K

Silent, as in knowledge but not kiss, knife but not kill;
and hard at work everywhere: kyrie, joke,

Kikuyu, kickback, blood-dark track, third strike.
You see that last K strung out over the upper deck

by the shirtless and drunk, a row tolling the fanned.
There and in the scorebook, it's marked backwards—

a child's mistake—to note those caught looking,
the fooled, frozen, or slow. Who cares why?

Set down, punched out, you walk off. Don't look back
toward the crowd, whatever cracks they make. Jerks.

However hard you're booed, you too know
it's like you threw a fight, stood there, got KO'd.

Lyric

So let that photo freeze you where you are,
your mouth skewed wide, as if sneering in song.
Let each thing in the frame stay where it is.

How else will you hold on? That moment,
not meant to be saved, is a little salvation.
If you ever thought

you could plan your life, could lay it out
like a schedule for travel, every day
taught you otherwise. The pimiento cheese

sandwiches your mother made
and placed in the blue cooler for the long drive
back in 1954 are still fresh. Below Asheville,

she hands each child half a sandwich—cool,
the way you like it—and you look out
the window as you eat, at the fast smear of colors

that you are, though you don't know it yet.

Mad

What if I turn right, not left, or if I walk straight,
or stop and look up? What if I cross the Oconee or I don't?
What if I look down at the water, at the paper trash
snagged in the weeds, or focus on the slow drift,
or close my eyes, or try to follow crows swooping down
out of the black gum? Not "What is the meaning
of my life now?" but "What's that odd shape
I am becoming?" Somebody help me. Am I empty?
Better empty than nauseated by some trickery or tacky
tick-tock mockery of time? Better blank than sick?
Lock onto the aisles of Shakespeare, dead as any man.
Onto everyone in oblivion. Galileo. Joe Louis. Jesus,
dead as a fried fish. Plato nowhere. And Ava Gardner,
where has she gone? Light from the wet street, a streaked
whetstone cold gray flash of blackwater and early sky,
looking-glass asphalt, no sidewalk. Chicken hours,
rooster eye. Why not crow out what can't be held back?
Mad hisses of lab cats in grainy old films, mouths fixed
in sham rage, cute bellhop caps screwed into the skull, all
electrodes alive now, and no way to choose. No way.

Message

Meth freak from way back, he wrote out endless notes
for the ceremony, and when the day comes,
his widow (who won't be long—she's wired too, bony

as Simone Weil) plays "Whipping Post," the long version,
on the boom box, and Leon Russell's
"Ballad for a Soldier," chosen for the refrain:

Stray dogs that live on the highway walk on three legs
cause they move too slow to get the message. Yes.
And there she is, dancing her little crippled strut up front.

"He didn't want nobody talking about God, didn't want
nobody to cry." But she violates
both those wishes with her last words, sobbing them out:

"And I'll be goddamned
if I know what else to say about the man. I mean,
he was one of a kind." And the folks in the folding chairs,

ready to go home, most of them, say "Amen."

Never

Christ, right there,
headless on his cross. Bottles and beer cans

strewn all over, ghost-litter, though the dead
don't party. They are far too cool. All day,

they're laid back, easy in their graves. So what
if the locomotives rock them, if the trees

ignite, flash and wave, if the season
is a species of news? Do the dead ever rise?

Tell the truth: who knows? But to me,
this is our beyond. I look around

at the ether of nothing,
the nowhere that we are traveling through,

and the everlasting never that might have been.

Night

My wife's down the hall, already in bed.
I have dozed off
here in my recliner, the TV bright but mute.
I struggle up to make my little tour.
I check the locks and turn off the lights,
but at the computer, I take a seat.
My son holds his daughter in the photo.
She's eight months old.
Both meet my eyes evenly, as if to say,
"Only the straight truth now, old man,"
and I can't move. In my son's face,
I see love. Forgive me. I see time. I do.
But in hers—
world that was, world that is, world to come.
The screen saver times on, a field of stars,
and I am traveling, as though on a spacecraft
or a planet, but alone, out into the night.
Then, like I'm God,
I move my hand, and there they are again.

Obituary

Derrida is dead. That's the word,
yet who knows, now, how to read

even the headlines, let alone the obituaries?
Today, in Derrida's notice, there is a photo

of the man at ease in his reading place,
and along one fold of the curtain behind him,

a curl of light. But look again. The reflection
is a flaw that you can follow

out of the image, into the text below,
down through words marred by faint print—

this accident that makes it all the way
to the bottom edge of section A, page 26.

Plot

Say the clouds held Ezra Pound's face for a while,
until his mouth grew wide, as though with pain,
and his fluffy head drifted into watery blue.

Say your life had a plot.

Say you drove all night, caught Jackie Wilson clear
on some local AM near Birmingham,
but lost him, so you stopped and went to sleep.

Say you woke up scared;

you drove away fast, and when the fog raced out
onto the blacktop, shapeless in front of the car,
you turned on the radio, rolled down the windows,

and you thought your life was over, though the choir
on the radio told you it was not.

Praise

When I heard the learn'd astronomer,
I realized I'd walked into the wrong lecture, so I left

and wandered the halls, finally asked someone
for the right room. And there it was, the wilderness,

already on the screen when I sat down. Hallelujah
for the ions, messiahs out of never. Let the species

say Amen. Let every human
give praise to the membrane, the delicate skin

of the spirit. And to the stars, yes, forever out there,
but we are here, still, in our only time,

humbled by our own cells, our little travels, our
Easters of each day. We are the very

electrons of the uncanny. We are the liquid, tricky
beats that we can't keep up with. Salt of love,

O little thought,
how excellent you are, slowed down, here in the dark.

Promise

Those back roads traveled me all my life.
Time spent me in idleness, wasted me.

Small towns passed through me, the old
melodies put me on and played me,

and stars used me to reckon with.
Maybe the truth tried to find me out.

A little history learned me. Right away,
it forgot. An odd dream, here and there,

understood me. The same old stories
told me over and over, and my soul

tried to save me, until
the day night walked off into me, alone,

when a promise broke me.

Question

Who among you, if his son asks for an egg,
will give him a scorpion? Does this offend you?
Where is your father? Where are my brothers?

Why did you look for me? Why are you crying?
Who touched me? Who among you,
if his son asks for a fish, will give him a snake?

How is it that you do not understand?
You come out, as though I were a thief,
with all your weapons?

Why are you giving this woman such trouble?
What are you saying to each other,
with such sadness? Will you go away too?

Do you realize what I have done to you?

Risen

Out of lightning soup; up out of the slop
of God; out of how many eons of light

like skin on the pond; out of the southpaw
amino acids; out of how many tides;

out of bubbles that held; out of cell walls;
out of the old apes' days and nights, parties

where they whooped it up; out of their sleep
interrupted; out of standing up,

and out of the upright, too—preach, brother;
out of fingertips, out of lifting up,

out of the soft grip, the delicate letting go;
out of God knows what, we have all risen

far enough to laugh, and to fall. But risen.

Sunday

Sunday evening. The sun coming out
as it goes down,

the wet leaves of white oak blown into light,
a sweet floating of tea rose through the windows,

and it's all a soft drifting away,
a far-off, easy blues. The long shadows

lose their clean lines,
and the body of every weed, each blade of grass,

fades, one by one,
to tintype, slipping into the past.

Tennessee

But there will come a time
when the jar out there on the hill says nothing at all;

when the jelly jar, scoured of every sweet molecule,
or the widemouth pickle jar, words pressed into its side,

lies there as wild
as the blind salamander that crawls all over it,

and whatever those words once said,
they can say that no more. Take the plain Mason jar

delivered to my father's table the year he died.
Or take the headstone engraved with 1989.

Take the grave itself, any grave, or the road, or the sky.
There will come a time when each of these

has no way at all
to mean. There will be no Tennessee. Say a house

settles and creaks, as if set adrift.
It will hold no sadness. In that wild place, there will be

no wilderness.

Timing

A coffee shop off Wabash.
Not a wash of traffic, but a broken-field running of it,
not a sea of humanity, but a secret

choreography. I sit here
waiting for my daughter,
and what is this malaise? I think of Del Close,

the Chicago comedian who willed his skull
to the Goodman Theatre as Yorick, asking only
to be listed in the credits,

as he always is. She's late,
but a sparrow alights inside the sidewalk cafe
and makes its way straight to me,

hitting its mark onstage, and she's crossing the street.

Toast

Here's to the freestyle plighting of the troth—

nuptials in free fall, weddings in the aisle
at the ball game. Let us raise a glass

to anyone who does take another

for better or worse, but underwater,
or perhaps atop a Ferris wheel or fire tower,

or floating on the lake. Let us drink
to those who will always have Elvis

and Memphis, and that figure on the cake.

True

There is an order called True Bugs—
this, to distinguish them

from the beings commonly called bugs
that are not, such as beetles,
the largest order in all the kingdom.

When I was a child, Clarence Chancey,
a grown man, rode his old bike
all over town. Everyone knew him

as True Friend, since he'd greet you,
whoever you were, with those words,
true friend, the way you might shout,

"Hey, kill that bug," but it's a beetle.

2

It's the first cool evening of fall

when the bowl of light—the high school field,
seen from the highway—almost compels
the night to surround it, but does not.

You drive on—this is not your town,
not even your autumn—with no thought
of leaving the road, rolling to the parking lot,

44

letting down the windows
for the woodsmoke and mowed field, the old
off-key warbling of the bugles, because

a true note is still so hard to hit.

3

Graveside. The sky did threaten. *The Lord
is my shepherd, I shall not . . .* At that word,
rain hit hard, quick as a fall

on a slick floor. The preacher had to shout.
That this is all true does matter. Aunt Reba
had a crazy fear of rain all her life.

After Vasco died, if she saw a cloud
that worried her, she would head out
to a niece's house or a nephew's. And after

years of this, the rain made us uneasy too.
But true to God: with the words
my cup runneth over, the canopy opened

and dumped the rain weighing it down—
buckets of it, that fast, it was a biblical rain—
onto the first row, onto those of us

closest to her.

Understanding

1

There's always Charles Whitman,
who—before he crushed the back of his mother's head
     and smashed her hands and stabbed her with a hunting knife;
before he returned home and stabbed and killed his wife too;
before he climbed the tower
     at the University of Texas with a high-powered rifle
     and shot sixteen dead and wounded thirty-eight;
before they shot him twice in the head with a twelve-gauge—

had written note after note to himself, trying to control his anger;
had gone to a psychiatrist;
had turned himself in to the police, had asked them,
     without success, to arrest him;
had suffered bad headaches that never eased off;
had written that he didn't understand
     his violent thoughts, or "any specific reason for doing this";
had asked that the autopsy study his brain.
     (They found the tumor.)

There's always Charles Whitman, God in his tower,
     answering his pain.

2

They found him in a twenty-dollar room, slumped across
the bed, frilly garters still in place,
so his death became a joke. There he was,

his whole life attired in flamingo pink,
his every conversation, each pause and careful word
tangled in the silky lingerie,

and even those who loved him understood
the small town's oddly pleasant mood,
and why a smile came quickly when the talk

returned to the middle-aged man
who was a member of the church, who'd displayed
Hank Snow's picture on his wall,

whose red truck everybody knew, and who once
wrote a short, angry letter to the county paper,
saying we should all wake up, this is still

America; whose hand people grabbed
on the street after that, having not the least doubt
what he meant.

Village

Only their ghost-song haunts the field—

a line from Kunitz, who taught in this town
briefly, and who stood here

on this mound built by the Mississippians
a thousand years ago. You can see the town

across the river. A single crow
throws its raw croak over the Ocmulgee,

and there is nothing for me to say.
I see my shadow, foolish totem, far below.

I spread my arms wide. I hold them out
for a moment. Why not?

Villanelle

Brother, I'm trying here for a poem
that's got some humor in it.
I know you're dead, son, but help me out.

All those years, I tried to write
my "Big Bad Villanelle," using those lines
out of "Samaritans," from your first book.

But that didn't work out either, did it?
Shit, Larry, I'm dying here.
Woman at the bar slams down her beer can.

"I done changed my mind," she says.
"I'm gonna stay here with you. I love you."

Wrong

I'm changing clothes at the gym, headed home,
when I overhear two men talking
beyond the next row of lockers.
"We're both doing all right, I guess." The three of us
are alone in the locker room, late evening.
The other voice, halting and awkward:
"Not something you just get over, I know that,
if you ever do." A metal door
whines and bangs shut. "No, it's not.
Not when it's your own child." I'm tying my shoes.
"*You* ought to go before they do."
I'm dressed now. "He had a little boy
himself, you know, three years old. He's a pistol."
I hear a chuckle. I hear the ache inside it.
I stand, and I feel for my keys.
"How's his wife doing?"
A man runs in, curses at the clock, and rushes out.
I sit back down. What's wrong
with a man like me who will do this,
sit back down so he can listen? "Better than I am,
I guess. Went out to his house
the other day"—the voice sticks in his throat—
"and there was his old truck. I stood there and cried."
The quiet hardens. The other man,
the good friend, waits. And finally, he says,
"Just broke down, huh?" And the bereaved father:
"No, it cranked right up."
I'm on my feet now, hustling out the door.
I'm fighting my way home through the heavy air.

X

Eyes of the dead; antepenultimate
spot in the alphabet; opposite of the check mark,

not the answer; axis along which
each boat, large or small, travels; ray that reveals

secrets of the bones; so many lost names
from the Yoruba and the Igbo; z-sound;

voiceless velar fricative; every kind of unknown;
word of the illiterate;

written in us all, the female chromosome;
the unnamed supreme; reactance; extra; erasure;

a kiss. What you solve for.

Young

Out in that field,

he tried to speed up time, surprise his own shadow,
set foot on his head—the criterion for noon,

when he could start out for the house to eat.
He tried to fake out his own shape, step on his hat

early. His brothers laughed
when they saw him jump sideways and turn

and stab the dirt with his bare foot,
or make a little stutter-step hesitation move, as if

he could deceive it, that exact
and contrary shade the sun made him.

Zero

Denominator that makes us uneasy, element
of identity, point so remote

no arrow can reach it, not the one
that shot the hole through it. Here too

is the low comedy of aught over naught,
of everything partialed out by nothing; here

is our vessel of oblivion, money for the dead;
whatever there is, minus itself; coefficient

of all our truths. Here is the ruthless
holder of place, multiplier of hours, a cipher.

But this too: nobody's mouth, soundless
with laughter.

TWO. From *Somewhere in Ecclesiastes*

Notes for a Prayer in June

FOR GLENN HAWKINS JR.

I

                      The other boys lived,
and a prayer grew from this:
the unbelievable sadness of chance
and the shattering dazzle of glass still strewn,
days later, on the road.

2

My son won't let things go, and I love
his fighting to understand, in his own terms.
Having learned about light years, he recalled
the distance to the school, how heavy
his legs felt when he raced there.
                      What form
will his knowledge of the wreck take,
when he learns how, late one Sunday,
twenty Junes ago now, I flung you from the world,
through a windshield?
                  Will I tell him
how I ran to get help,
yet tired, had to slow down, my legs turned to lead,
had to rest in the face of death, how far
I have traveled through the years?

3

I remember the late spring night we camped out
on Alcovy Mountain, just the three of us
who later on would take that ride.
We laughed at ourselves for playing war.
We were nearly sixteen.
And it seems like a last act of childhood,
crawling up the north slope
so softly I could reach for a branch,
draw a bead down its gnarled barrel
and laugh you dead.
                        The next morning
when absolute darkness had failed, for a while,
we stood without words above the world,
a white mist drifting far beneath us
forever, over homes we were headed for.

4

Is it breath rising in the Christmas air
as a child pedals up and down the driveway at dawn?
Is it dizziness with which
a woman has to reach for the words
to send into silence with her son?
                        Each June,
it's the brief taste of salt, licked away,
as a boy hurries out to the street, having breezed
through the hot kitchen, kissed his mother's face.

5

Before our eyes, that heavy old coin disappears,
while it stays where it is. We're aware
sundown is a lie now,
though we see it the same. Chimpanzees
pause, sometimes, from their foraging or play,
sit quietly and gaze into the west
until moved by darkness.
                              Perhaps, in their eyes,
nothing seems magical, or it all does. From us
comes a forced, final nod toward the sleight
of relentless method, how it turns
pure mystery to laughter in the end.
                              Still,
we know there's a magic we begin with, tricked
by love's act into this ruled world.

Wonder

It can start with nearly anything, the delicate theme
of a late-night talk show or the desperate, false
laugh track of a bad sitcom. Sometimes,
I see us all sitting here
lulled off forever by a gas leak, and the TV
still selling us deodorants and beer, selling lies
about our lives. I want to turn
from the dead screen able to say
this life is a holiness, it is all we will have.
I want to load us into an Oldsmobile
with windows that won't roll up, upholstery
musty from years in the garage. I want to ride,
washed with the summer air's warm velvet cloth,
ride to where the stars come clear, where the road
goes from blacktop to concrete slab, sudden dirt.
I want to trouble dust for miles, till we roll
to a hill overlooking a farm,
where a long gold light floats out in a field
like a lost ray of sun, where the cattle lie buoyed
by the earth, their heavy spines curving over hearts
slowing in the drift toward sleep. I want to feel
how the old car trembles and dances and kicks,
trying not to die, then click the lights off,
kill the engine, and listen
to the tree frog, cricket, and cicada staccato,
the soft lows rising, as in wonder, from the darkness,
as if asking, repeatedly, *What are you doing here?*
Why are you here?

The Touch

FOR MY MOTHER

You stepped out the back door, drying your hands
on a plain white apron
and watching me slap the new basketball down
on the driveway's nearly flat hardpan,
unable to control it or to stall,
for long, its falling still.

You held out clean, wrinkled hands for the ball,
let it drop and caught the rise
with the fingertips, never with the palm,
allowing no sound but the ball's hollow bounce,
crouching low, either small hand
moving *with* the ball.
                    And years later,
when the Newton County Rams came down,
like the cavalry at dawn on a few Cheyenne,
in a hot-breath man-to-man press, the best plan
was to get the ball to me. Even now,
I return to that late fall morning
when you taught me what a softer touch could do,

how to go where I needed to, never looking down.

Laments

FOR A SMALL BOY, CONFUSED ABOUT WORDS,
AT THE AUCTION OF HIS HOME

What country are these folks from, you wonder,
who follow the machine-gun nonsense
the man on the truck bed talks, these folks
who are whispering words you know,
like *whiskey* and *pity* and *wife*.
                         But how
can a man really drink away a farm?
You imagine the fish pond tilted like a cup,
all the cows guzzled dry,
the milk barn, farmhouse, miles of barbed wire,
and the John Deere melting like a sliver of ice
on the highway's soft tar in August.
                              Nothing
remains unswallowed but the sky
which surrounds you now, wherever you stand,
like a glass turned upside down.

FOR A MAN WHO CARRIES HIS LOVER'S
BABY PICTURE IN HIS WALLET

You follow the full moon home, so empty
you ease off onto the shoulder
of the shortcut you always take, cut the engine

and listen to the hot block tick
like a heart too irregular to live with.
Again, you look at the snapshot

you carry for her mouth, the trace of icing
on the lower lip slightly pushed forward, as if
she begins just then to be sad. And it hurts

that the baby's not looking at the camera,
that the beautiful, Bible-dark eyes gaze off,
forever, past the one who is holding her.

FOR AN OLD MAN WHO CAN'T
REMEMBER HIS MOTHER'S FACE

Your left breast pocket's still vivid with its medal
of day-old egg, and your pants
sag like a clown's flowered trousers, or those
of a man living alone, no woman to reflect on,
with something like cancer—but it's not that—
eating his weight.
                    You shuffle to a seat
in the corner, by the last snooker table
at Freddy Bray's shotgun pool room.
A fight kicks up without warning. A cue stick
kisses your cheek in a backswing, leaves you
lapping up the powdery dust, the crisp hulls
of insects swept to the wall.
                    You know
she expects you to come straight home after school.
She's forgotten what it was to be a girl, all day
ironing in other folks' homes. You can feel
her hands moving over your clothes, making sure
the creases are sharp when you start out. Now,
you struggle up onto your feet,
                         and you think
of her eyes when she sees this blood on your shirt.   63

Rocking Anna to Sleep

It was almost sorrow, what I used to know
as a child, not wanting to drift off,
hearing the even, deep breaths
of my brother, to whom
everything was lost: the cracked door's
line of pure light climbing the wall,
far down Church Street, a solitary bark
catching on, even the cool pillow,
its familiar smell.
                    The small breaths
of the girl failing in my arms
grow slower and deep. I think of how
she trails this worn blue nylon nightgown
all over the house. She loves
the feel of one button. But I know
if I lifted her hand,
it would easily open and fall back
free as a raindrop.
                    The rocker's soft
creak keeps time. I let it die.
And perhaps she's startled by the change
or has gone so far in her dreams,
she can say—by tightening her grip
when I pull at the gown—*you are wrong
if you think there is nothing in the world
you can always hold.*

Night Ride, 1965

Exactly at one o'clock,
I crawl out, walk the half mile to the dirt road,
wait for the loud DeSoto, its gold now sanded dull brown,
color of damp pine straw. When the car slows,
dust catches up, steams forward through the headlights,
into the dark. The farm station signed off for hours,
all the others too remote for the aerial,
the radio's faint rasped harmony's lost
to the car's bass throb. As we cross the main road,
we can look down at the small town's single row of stores,
streetlights blazing like a runway
only the desperate or crazed would try to land on,
and we cruise all night down narrow county roads,
talking as though we could say it all, could tell
what it means to grow quiet at the first light,
while the stars all fail, what it means
finally to turn home
with the clear crackle of tires rising from the wet road,
as sweet cut fields come cool through rolled-down windows.

On the Otis Redding Bridge

Macon, Georgia

This morning, when a woman walks home
from the graveyard shift at the cotton mill;
when she comes to the Otis Redding Bridge, coughing,

and turning her head, so the snowflake dust
on her shirt whirls off through a sheer gold sleeve
the early sun lays across the road,

        what I need
is the voice of Otis Redding—

and the power that would let a man shout
sanctified, tender, and sad, let him cry,
angry, yet shocking in his praise.

          I want to sing
the cotton dust caught in the sunlight;
and the woman who is not slowed down in the least
by the momentary beauty that began

as an old pain deep in her lungs; this woman
who spits off the bridge and goes on.

Home

The TV's white noise
hisses me back, this first
awareness the worst one: lights on,
wine by the bed, stale cigarettes,
chicken box greasy on the Gideon,
an hour before dawn. The orange moon
on the far wall's dull watercolor
is nowhere in the lake.

I remember my father's game.
Having come from the mill,
settled in his chair, he would tell us
that the game was on. Unseen,
either he had hidden
something in plain sight—
pencil in a flowerpot—
or changed things slightly,
setting the clock back
or taking a knob off the radio.
He knew how simple it was
and watched us, giving no clue.

When the trucker overhead slams home,
his kicked-in turquoise door
not catching, the chain on mine
rattles. I recall
there was never a prize back then.
There was only the seeing.

Playground in the Rain

The rain falls hard, straight as chains
the worn, still swing seats hang on,
and the slide flares darkly, its blade
clattering as though each sound it has known
could return—each loose, ticking shoestring,
every open coat rapping metal buttons,
a buckle or a zipper. In the hollows
by the seesaw, underneath the swings, in the bare
circle at the jungle gym, puddles form.
The horses have lost their eyes to the weather,
waiting in a perfect line. Their guts
give a thick dark coil to the mud.

I think of how things go wrong,
how Janice Scott suddenly dropped limp
through a tangle of bars, how the seesaw
caught Leon Dillard under the chin,
shattered his jaw, broke teeth. And I think
of a boy we had cruelly called Baby Shoes because
he was small for the first grade,
who meandered in the path of a swing, as it arced
backwards as far as it could, then rode
the weight of a large child down to his temple.
I recall how the blood made beads in the dirt,
the children all gathered as quietly as clouds,
and the playground grew this still.
                                    I recall
how differently everything gleamed, as in rain,
the paths home, curves in the bars, those shoes.

In the Kingdom of the Air

By now, everyone knows there is nothing
in everything.
        How easily we see it
in the old man dragged by a self-propelled mower through his yard,
in a cloudy winter noon when a single leaf waves at the sun,
in the first quick smacks of the rain.
                   Maybe,
a thousand miles from anyone who loves you,
you encounter some woman who has stolen the face
of your mother, and she hurries on by.
                     I have stood
in the dark near a window
of a tall office building while a couple made love on a roof
several stories beneath. I could see
every privacy, the way
she twisted her mouth, how he fumbled and rushed,
then wrapped her in the blanket they had laid across the tar.

We have all seen a child's blue balloon floating low
and ghostly in the hall, losing helium.

But a woman turns sharply through an intersection.
The back door opens, and her two-year-old falls beneath the wheels
of the next car through. Who will fail
to inhabit that woman
as she drives away, completely unaware;
as she pulls down the visor, then frowns, realizing
she forgot to buy the milk; as she notices
the headlights flashing behind her?
                   Who,
turning, doesn't gather up the air, doesn't enter
the kingdom of the air?

Somewhere in Ecclesiastes

> The one who will not contend with realities gets phantoms
> to battle against. —Kierkegaard

I. ACCIDENT

A kitten, startled onto the stove, tips over
a pan of boiling water.
And a little boy, weakened by his burns, must surrender

to pneumonia, must become
a piece of deep blue in the puzzle
his mother hasn't yet put together. He is sky,

surely, but the kitten—what is it?
A diagonal of rain? Does she have to fit it in—
the streak of soft gray? Who will tell her?

Her friends have faith in mysterious ways.
They say it, and they say it, until God
himself kicks the handle of the pan. And for her,

all the colors turn ugly and cruel unless
there is chaos at the root of every beauty—she is wild,
remembering his eyes—and we are blessed

only by accident, only by chance.

What if it were true, after all,
that the body is a garment, a light cotton shirt
we will easily do without?

If we knew this beyond any question,
would it alter the funerals of children?
                                    Imagine
a world in which the mother of a seven-year-old
who was killed in a wreck doesn't come
from the new grave feeling like a woman

who struggles up out of a lake, soaked,
wearing everything she owns,
and who can't take anything off, not a scarf,
not a ludicrous hat with a feather.
                                    What
if the body were a silk slip lifted in the hands
of a lover, then tossed on the floor,
with a laugh?

3. MAN

While the dust rolls in from the road, he remains
by the open front door of the gas station,
sitting on a turned-up Coca-Cola crate,

as though he has been there forever, as though
there is no other home he can go to.

If you gesture, headed for the door, he will nod,
slightly, in return. He will raise one hand
to his greasy red baseball cap, whose bill
is pulled down low, so he has to lean back
to look you in the eye, if he chooses to.

He chain-smokes cigarettes, dropping the butts
in the two long swallows of beer grown hot
in the bottle at his feet. He imagines
the back of your neck in the crosshairs
as you walk toward your car; or he thinks

of calling out "Wait"—then telling, again,
if he can, what happened to his son.

You have seen this man. He appears,
like the dust caught loitering in air by the late
afternoon sun, anywhere.

4 . SON

This is all routine,
but I can't stop watching you and taking in details:
the first, barely visible growth
of fine, dark hair on your upper lip;

your lanky frame's angles, revealed
by the one thin sheet; the foot sticking out
has a half-moon callus on its ball;
and the profile—flattened at the nose, badly broken
just a few hours back by an elbow.

You don't even flinch when the nurse
jabs in the needle, but it leaves me thinking
of a morning last week when I saw
a yellow jacket writhing in a shroud, caught
by a spider which had climbed on its victim
and was thrusting in its poison. I remember

that the rhythm seemed to build to a shudder
as the spider pulled away;
the yellow jacket's panic disappeared, so he lay
in his silver-white hammock of silk, rocked
by the breeze. And your eyes glaze over. I am sure

this is all routine: the curtains have begun
to shimmer like the fall sun glancing off water;
and now, when I try to hold your hand,
you shake me off and smile, tiredly, going under.

Heaven is a ghost town. No one remains
where the road dead-ends into desert. At noon,

rattlesnakes cool their skins in the dark
lobby of the old hotel. A letter
yellowed in a drawer says "Everyone's fine,
and the good Lord willing . . ." then it blurs.

There's a baby doll swaddled in cobwebs
on a board rotting through in the mercantile,
a cry still poised in its throat. *Mama*

is the word it will call only once
if the shelf lets go. The weathervaned roof
of the one-room school's fallen in. The whine
of the wind turns mockingly human.

6. MORNING

When I walked out back with my coffee
to investigate a large red flower
sprouting in the uncut grass, I discovered

it was really two tall spider lilies
whose blossoms were entangled,
they had grown so close. Reaching under,

I broke one stem, and its bloom
hung cradled in the petals of the other.

And soon after dawn this morning,
a neighbor's cat bent to a pothole
in the driveway. A pale blue shimmered

in the puddle's black sheen, as the cat
glanced over at the rustle of my paper.
She held my eyes for a while,

then turned back, slowly, to the hole
and lowered her mouth to the sky.

To sleep late, eat a light breakfast, and step,
leisurely, into the sun;

to smooth on coconut oil and recline
on a soft, thick towel, then cultivate the calm
simplicity of the gulls
that sail down low over the wet, glassy sand,
undisturbed by their reflections.

                      Later on,
to drink a little wine and eat a sandwich
in the room. Though it's cool,
to turn the air high, then ease in under
the covers, reaching over to the night stand
for the Gideon. To let it fall open, at random,
somewhere in Ecclesiastes,

                  and to sleep.
To wear a white Panama hat on the beach
and a painful new skin. To be finishing
a paperback mystery greasy with oil,
a deeply flawed novel, still compelling
with unexplained death.

There is a time to heal, and a time to cast away,
to turn each page with an absolute faith.

When the long drought broke, we sat on the front porch, watching
in silence, as if
it were any other rain, while the sheets of dark silver hissed down
on the hot blacktop.
We could smell the rain washing through the corn, ten acres
of dwarfed brown stalks we would soon plow under.

When we all ate supper at my uncle's house,
my great-grandmother had forgotten, again,
her own son's name. The simplest things—
utensils and napkins, the passing of bowls—
easily confused and defeated her.

But my grandfather told us a story:
when Jack's Creek flooded years ago,
a Guernsey had swum, unharmed, all the way
down to Highway 11, then strolled into town—
as haughty as Geraldine Phillips, he said,
and snorting when it walked, just as she did.

Hearing that comparison, my grandfather's mother
started laughing. She cackled so intensely
her upper plate floated in her mouth, nearly clattered to the table,
and her pale skin reddened, and she rocked, shaking hard,
till her son had to take her in his arms.

We had all gone limp in our straight chairs, wiping back tears,
when she quit, falling quiet once again. And we sat
listening to the rain.

9. POEM

I'm seduced by a poem that can move
like a beautiful woman,
sultry in her black silk dress. She will step

through the soft, golden lighting of a restaurant,
assuming she has lowered our voices—and she has—
as we follow her return from the ladies' room.
She is elegance and style
                                    until she whirls,
discovering a light green, three-foot banner
of toilet paper trailing from her right high heel.

But I am searching for a poem that redeems
like an elderly widow
living in the country by herself. She's aware

of every little sound; she is frightened by the wind
cutting through a locked screen door, by the hoot
of an owl, too deliberate and low. Every night,
she will lay a small pistol and a dog-eared Bible
by her pillow, just to feel

the smooth, empty chamber of his favorite, to inhale
the tobacco in the paper, and to fear
nothing she remembers then, and nothing she can hear.

10. DESIGN

The swallows wheel off through the aisles, as if
they are set free here,
within this design. I have always loved

the strict, dark geometry of pecan groves,
those cathedrals of shade:
the clean, hushed acres of shadow, the cool

avenues of dusk,
the bare, neural branches in the late fall
reaching through the fog, or as though

delicately traced, in India ink,
on the shadings of red in a sunset.
And the small, quick flocks of the swallows—

I have loved those too, how they move
beneath one skin
the color of the breeze, with only one thought

rising when they billow and fall. And tonight,
they have spiraled all over the grove.
They have settled in the matrix of trees, as if

euphoric, released, all talking at once.

Explanations

A boy holds a blown glass sparrow in his hand
and can't resist testing one finger against
a clear, fragile wing. When it gives,
the child looks up at his mother. As if
to revise what has happened, he explains:
he didn't press hard enough to snap it. The crippled
figure is to blame.

                And when Nietzsche went insane,
when he buried his bushy face deep in the neck
of a horse whipped hard in the street, of course
there was someone to haul out the photograph
of Nietzsche himself hitched up to a cart
driven by the woman he had loved, the young
Salome wielding a whip.

                    I remember
Jesus' explanation to his puzzled disciples
of his speaking in parables. Otherwise, he said,
the heathen would understand too, and they
would also be saved. I have always believed
Jesus had a zany sense of humor.

                     Consider
the way we are taught and defeated, at once,
when a thought angles back on itself,
as when Plato alleges that Socrates lies
with every single word from his mouth, and then
Socrates owns up, holding, with a smile,
that Plato has spoken the truth.

                              I recall
my son and his best friend, each one lost
in his own loud monologue, rolling their battered
matchbox cars down the driveway.
My son said, "History can start any time."
And his friend fell silent, appearing to ponder
how history is born,

then shook his head yes,
as though he had understood fires and freak wrecks,
leukemia and early, slow death well enough
to start off walking down the hill, not saying
just anything he happened to think of.

About Women

Who is more foolish than the poor man
who tries to give his son the honest truth
about women?
                    When the boy is thirteen,
the man thinks back to how the world had to change,
how its giving curves began to fill him up,
and he wants to tell his son what it is
he has learned since then, what women
might mean in his life.

So he tells the boy Paul was surely wrong
when he said to the Corinthians
if a man could get by, not touching a woman,
that was good. He relates how Freud
died, still baffled by females. He pulls in
Darwin to explain why everyone turns
to watch a certain girl walk by.
                            And he talks
of Saturday mornings, when the sun slants in
through the bedroom window,
how his wife comes warm into his arms
to share the way the dust luxuriates in light,
to lie there and listen to the house as it settles,
to the rustling of children in the next room,
and to drift back, together.
                        But he thinks
of something he will keep to himself:
his desire for a woman at the beach last year.
She was old, slightly bent, not beautiful.
Her housedress trailed through the foam, gaped open
to the waist.

He is puzzled, uneasy,
remembering his daughter
in the mornings, how he finds her, tightly curled,
shivering, the quilt kicked off. How she wakes
facing any wall, turned at random, as if spun
like a bottle, unaware, though she has dreamed.

What You Have Need Of

Again, the stars gathered like children at dark
into light, taken like the clearest of dreams
into quiet, yet there, you are gone.

Once, the old *World Book* still tucked under your arm,
you led me into a field, away from the lights of houses,
to show how the whole figures are not there,
and therefore, you draw your own lines, how then
you can link what's scattered into anything.

And what you have need of flares in that far
eternity that dies too, quiet village of the universe.

Tonight, when sleep, failing, has fallen into old grief,
I have walked out into the back yard, hearing that voice,
and waited where the land slopes downward miles
to the town's lights, a clear lake raised to the stars,
darkness floating on the far last ripple of streetlights.

There are those who defeat their dreams, who know,
when the brother of childhood stands in the doorway,
not to believe, but I am not one.

Where We Are

Coals raked out on hearthstones writhe like men.
Lake weeds resemble a madonna, and great rocks
erode into profiles, smiling at clown-faced clouds
or frowning, puzzled as they peer far down
at long-dry streambeds, unable to find old light.
Blossom, starfish, mandrake, shadows in snow
open their arms. Everywhere, eyes spiral:
in the leaves of water lilies they are amazed,
in slow creeks' vortices sleepy, a little sad,
in wood grain knowing, nearly sensual, in wings
of hawk moths, blind. And hands are found in coral,
ears in shells, the small breasts of young girls
in tree trunks, skulls in walnuts. But faces
draw us as though we were infants: to chrysalids
swaying on the underside of leaves, to sawn marble
and photos of the surface of Mars, to ice melting
an old man into the wind, to hollow, dead trees
and shacks blank-eyed on hills. There is also Christ
burned into hearths, into cloth, photographed
in thunderstorms, forest fires, waterfalls, and found
gentle in walls, the torn asbestos of a henhouse,
lichen of cathedrals. But this is not enough.
There's the taste of dust churned up from a dirt road
a wrecked pickup has rattled down, late summer,
the dusk like cooling iced tea, almost too sweet,
and the truck's wake coaxing a crushed wing upward.
There is rippling lake light slowing, how blackbirds
coil far off like smoke, shadows of small clouds
sailing in the fields. Always, there is rain,
its slow coming on in a heavy, ticking stillness,
how it sounds on the old barn's dark tin roof

or dripping from trees afterwards, when steam
curves ghostly along the blacktop, and new skies
gather in puddles. There are paths followed
at dawn through grazed fields flaming with dew,
the paths worn smooth as the handles of old tools.
And fireflies floating through the night, brief smells
of plowed earth caught through diesel, or colors
of sundown fallen in the hills, the cool air
sharpened with coal smoke, dark coming early,
when something is found.

Nature

We, who are last year's dust and rain . . .
—Loren Eiseley

1

Men of science knew it in their bones, that if light
travels at the speed of God, only one thing
in the universe could match it—

a human thought shooting through the nerves.
But who could get a reading? The velocity
easily would equal that of starlight. Yet,

when Helmholtz measured the speed
of the impulse, he chuckled. Even though
the metaphor remains *illumination*, we're aware

an idea arrives like a child
who plays hard all afternoon, self-involved,
who somersaults off across the yard, who discovers

it's dark before he knows it.

2

There's a yellow moon low over the parking lot.

My son, seventeen, points it out
as we slam the trunk shut on the groceries.
"Look at that."

We have held off work all day.
He played my old guitar, I read a novel,
and we have driven to the supermarket, set

to bring home only the necessities.
We stand here taking in the moon
through the earth's dusty lens, and I resist

giving anything but "yeah" as an answer.
When he holds out a hand for the keys, chooses
a longer route back to the house

and rolls too slowly down Maplewood Lane,
once nearly coming to a stop, he does not
explain. The yellow moon

follows us, whichever way we turn.

3

Maybe I am simply tired out by the drive,

but far up in the bleachers, when I hear
the high school's valedictorian
quoting Emerson,

if I let myself go, I could cry. A light breeze
sweeps through the humid June dusk. A woman
in the next row whispers, then returns

her attention to the amplified words.
But the wind picks up, until it billows
through the boy's purple gown, until he seems

an adolescent Moses, come to lead
his people to the wilderness, his voice
cutting like the scripture,

quoting Emerson. There is
the wind and how it sounds, like distant thunder,
blowing on the open microphone. Then there is

the thunder in the distance, and the difference.

4

We had to get a loan to cut it down.

Drought took several years to kill it, but then
limbs began to plummet
to the roof from a hundred feet up. Mr. Brown,

in the business all his life, gave his word
he had never cut a tree this big, then he wrote
an estimate far below the others.

He worked two days, with a crew of ten men,
on the red oak older than the country,
and he left the ground level. It was late

on the second afternoon when a few of those men
visited the truck for a pint of Old Crow.
The oak itself offered up the smell

of a strong, honeyed wine gone sour in the cask—
centuries of rain, the men agreed,
had fermented in the wood. And when they left,

we kept on standing in the yard, challenged
by the air, as if something
essential still needed to be done, but we

were only human.

Driving Home from the Clinic

On the narrow back road to Monroe, after rain,
the air was a bittersweet tea
of mayweed mixed with the creek, wild onion, and pine,
the freshly turned earth like a root split open,
then held to the nose.

I drove home slowly, with the windows rolled down,
and I listened to the hush of the tires
on the damp asphalt,
felt the patches of cool air washing my arm,

saw a farmhouse lighted by a single yellow bulb
and drifting far out in a field
as dark as the bottom of a lake, while the clouds
to the southeast blossomed with lightning.
                                        God,
it was all of this, even
the smell of a polecat killed on the road,
mingled with the wild sweet olive, this,
and the news,
that compelled me to know, for the first time,

that I want to grow old,
to entertain grandchildren, telling true stories
that surprise them at the end,
stories of things long past, yet to happen.
To be able to say:

The night it all started, there was jasmine
floating on the air.
There was mica in the wet road, glistening. Cicadas
had remembered how to sing.

A Knowledge of Water

I love the way the cows go down to the water
and wade in deep, till the nostrils rest
on the pond's copper film. In July,
when the oak shade bakes like a shut loft,
all the cattle walk off into coolness, feel
their heavy meat lift.
                              So the body
they drink from consumes them, becomes
a eucharist busy with flies. This stink
of pond slime, piss, and rotting possum
swallows till their giant taw eyes
gaze across the surface, where the light
changes every move.
                              And I believe
they can nearly take it in, like a drink—
the ripple, slope, fence, pines, sky—
and they walk from the pond onto earth
with a knowledge they will bear,
crossing dry pastures at dusk, single file,
their wet flesh heavier than before.

Loss of Power

The noon news chokes off, war in a man's throat.
The fan's blade quietly spins to a stop.
The bulb over a full sink fails. All this
happens at once, and a child shouts
"Hey" from the next room, comes
running to a man who is not surprised,
but oddly shocked, at the loss.
                              A mill worker,
a laid-off doffer in the card room who worked
sixteen hours routinely, he looks up
powerless to change this, and he thinks,
for the first time in his life, of the shape
the .38 would make in his pocket,
how no one would know him far away,
at a small bank in Ellijay
or a liquor store in Hartwell.
                              But tonight,
when his wife has laid out her tips on the steps,
far short of what Georgia Power wants,
he only walks, hands in his pockets, to the mill,
where he leans his forehead on the warm brick,
placing his palms on the trembling wall, feels
the power work through him like prayer.
For a long time, he stands like this.

Sunday Evenings

Sunday mornings seemed wrong for the soul,
so fragrant and perfect were the worshipers,
like a garden club arrangement of rare bulbs.
What I wanted was a field at dusk,
with dandelions leaning in the breeze.

In the evening there were always those
grown wildly alone. When Raymond
turned slowly into the aisle, leaned
doubled on his cane, unable to go on;
when Billy Reed's mother,
a sad, bent woman
who had gone so far into silence, sang,

then the world's true music touched ours,
all the windows of the old church open in June
to the mournful barks, fast whispers of tires.

The Beginning of Heaven

I have dreamed three times of my father
in the year since he died, yet twice he remained
faceless as a shadow:
having struggled from his bed,
he embraced me and vanished through a door;
and he waited like a beggar on the steps—
this was Thanksgiving night—but disappeared
when he tried to give his name.
                              Maybe dreams
were the origin of heaven:
say a man came back as himself,
not an actor in the theater of grief,
but the actual man, with his laughter, his walk;
unmistakably, his hands.
                              Close to dawn,
my father leaned back from the front seat,
holding three wrinkled five-dollar bills,
one for each child, and when his eyes—
absolutely his—grew amused
as we grabbed for the money; when he turned
and cleared his throat once, like a man
prepared to force everyone to listen,
but then simply reached for the key,

I believed we'd continue up the drive,
we'd complete that half mile ride to the fair,
the giant wheel visible, already, where we were.

Last Words

An old woman stands at the casket.
"Don't he look natural?" she asks.
I think about the phrase *of natural causes*,

how it indicates a different kind of violence.
I do know what she means,
and both of us admire the awful craft

of the worst undertaking in the world,
the taking under.
She turns from his petrified face. Raised

on her tiptoes, she whispers in my ear,
"I thought so much of your daddy." Odd
that I didn't really think of him at all,

or so it seems, now
that he's a riot in my head.
And everything he gave me,

which was everything he had,
I took that as a given. Only Saturday,
we talked on the telephone a while, but I can't

remember what he said.

Sunday

With six young blacks at the door of the church,
suddenly, in 1963,
and the preacher out of town, the decision
fell to you, as the chairman of the deacons.

You took them down the aisle, and I recall
you put them on the left, second pew,
in the same place Ben and I had waited,
at ages three and four, for the anthem
to be over. You would come down from the choir
to sit between us then.
                          I couldn't quit
glancing at the visitors,
who gave away nothing, not a trace
of the strain they must have felt.
                          That Sunday,
across the kitchen table, we agreed,
intensely, on the clarity of scripture:
"My house shall be a house of prayer . . .
all ye who labor and are heavy laden . . .
knock, and it shall be opened."

The congregation voted two to one
only one week later to exclude
Negroes from the services,

                              and soon—
confused by many things I couldn't name—
I would find this hypocrisy convenient
as the reason I would leave the Baptist Church
or any other faith. I made you pay
for staying on. What did I desire?

A man in a signboard trumpeting "Repent"
on the corner of the all-white church? Perhaps.
But I made this judgment from the sofa,
while watching old movies on the TV,
                                        reading
the fat Sunday paper,
starting with the comics and the sports.

2

A Sunday is a parable of time, always was.

In the hard-shell old days,
you couldn't drag a stick across the dirt.
The stick became a plow, the mark a furrow.

We heard those stories from your mother,
having traveled to her house after church, to sit,
forever, in the parlor, underneath
the portrait of a stern young man
at the center of the mantel.
                            Legend had it,
dancing got him turned out of the church.
Your father, in his coffin twenty years
when I was born, loved the mandolin
and the banjo that could bring him to his feet.

I like to think of that. And of the Sundays
when men played semi-pro ball on the mill field,
doubleheaders stretching into dusk,
into chimes coming soft over the pines, *sweet hour
of prayer.*

       Best of all, I remember
a pitcher with a slowness close to magical—
knuckleball, palm ball, sinker,
butterflies he fluttered at the batter.
                       Back then,
following the evening benediction,
often we would drive through the center of Monroe—
ghostly in its calm—
to the only place open, the Trailways station,
for the ice cream cones we had to eat

strategically and fast, that sweetness which began
melting as we took it in our hands.

3

This is partly explained, I am told, by the tricky
physiology of shock:
          I reacted
as though I had heard good news—a bizarre
confusion on a day of great clarity, with each
blossom of wild red clover, every breath
and bony arm sharply redefined. I had heard
my brother say thickly,

"He's gone."
                    There are those
who insist the word *love* explains nothing,
but is only a maneuver, like music, in the effort
to follow what the body figures out. Who has not
believed each move of a dream

till instructed by his name, or the daybreak? Who,
having reached my age, hasn't once
grown silent while the talk trickled on, got a look
at the faces of bone, then turned
with an ache to say it all?
                    Here's a story
I'd forgotten: early August in the Philippines, you
with CQ duty, while your buddies trucked off
to the show. Kay Kyser, at the close,
had stood with his arms wide, sobbing, to announce
it was over.
          So the men came back
dancing in the street, some choking out prayers
or running just to run, others quieter than ever,
observing themselves, oddly frightened.
                              When Ben

telephoned the news,
euphoria appalled me, joy washed over
my body. I'm unable to explain. I'd believe,
if I could, in the shock of sudden victory.
                              The only

word I have is *love*.

4

A sophomore stuffed with philosophy,
home from college on the weekends,
I cultivated arguments with you, attempts to show
the doubtful ontology of heaven.

Not arguments exactly—I would lecture, and you
would sit there listening, at times
asking me a question.
                    When the honeymoon
of grief left off, when I quit
letting go on the back road, headed for work,
or waking in the night, on my feet,
as if the telephone had rung,
                    I discovered
anger like a child's pure fury
at a simple recognition—the authority, say,
of gravity or sleep.
                    I am kneeling
at the grave, with a butcher knife in hand,
hacking at the dark fist of ice
that won't turn loose of the yellow silk flowers
we buried in the vase last summer.

Finally, it splits. Lynda kneels
with the bright poinsettia for the cylinder.

When you came to get us up, Sunday mornings,
for a few years there—it became a family joke—
you did it on cue:

the Lefevres sang "*I'll* Fly Away," signing off
a half hour of gospel on the radio. Why
do I think about this, still gripping the knife,

having nothing else to hit, with such a purpose?

5

Instead of heading home, one Sunday at noon,
we turned up 138, and we stopped
at a family place, east of Conyers.

But Mama didn't really have an appetite. To me,
it was army food—greasy, mass-produced.
The restaurant was hot, the lighting harsh,
the tables too close, and the single price high.

I took her to the other side of town,
to the small monastery she had never seen,
and neither had I, in the early afternoon,
when the sun angled down through the windows,
indigo and gold on the chapel floor.

A man walked alone through the sanctuary,
never looking up.
                         On the road
to Monroe, fields of goldenrod flickered
in the wind. When I wondered out loud
about the name of that weed,
she told me what it was, without surprise.

And I think about a morning at the old house,
of you and me looking at a spiderweb
delicate with light.
I reached out to tear the thing down,
and you caught me by the wrist.
                              If I believe

it was not a bright pain
that made your eyes open on a Sunday
in April, who will stop me? If I name

the day itself, the day of rest, the dust,

the silver-white filaments of dust floating down,
like a dream of falling snow,
through the avenue of light by the bed.
                              If I say

it was this that took your breath.

THREE. From *This April Day*

History of Rain

What if every prayer for rain brought it down?
What if prayer made drunks quit the bars, numbers hit,
the right girl smile, shirts tumble from the dryer
fully ironed? What if God

required no more than a word? Every spot
of cancer would dissolve like peppermint,
every heart pump blood through arteries as clean
as drinking straws then. All grief would be gone,

all reverence and wonder. But if rain
should fall only once in a thousand years, rare
as a comet; if, for fifty generations,
there was never that sweet hint of metal in the air

until late one April afternoon
when the dust began to swirl above the ball field,
and the first big drops fell, popping in the dirt,
and sudden as a thought, great gray-white sheets

steamed on the asphalt, fought with the pines,
would we all not walk out trying to believe
our place in the history of rain? We'd be there
for the shining of the world:

the weeds made gaudy with the quicksilver breeze;
the rainbows floating over black-glass streets;
each cupped thing bright with its blessing; and long
afterwards, a noise like praise, the rain

still falling in the trees.

Preface to an Omnibus Review

Do not write poems about poetry. Commit
no epigraphs, object poems, homages to anyone.
Please, no more elegies for your father. No details
of your grandmother's hands. Leave the sepia
photographs alone.
                Give us no
Guggenheim-and-here-I-am, bored-or-overwhelmed
poetry. Don't write about divorce—no ironic
meditations at the playground or the game.
Nothing on the limits of the language.
                      Construct
no ugly poems ragged on the page, but nothing square.
Go easy on the birds and the trees. No asleep-
in-the-deer-stand, waking-to-an-eight-point-buck-
only-thirty-yards-away kind of poetry.
                    And no
remember-that-cafe-in-San Diego poems
of heartbreak; not one Rilke imitation;
nothing modeled on the Spanish; nothing spoken
as Osip Mandelstam or Akhmatova.
                     If ever,
on a clear summer night,
there's a baseball diamond in a small town, a field
lighted like a scene in a glass paperweight,
an old man loud in the stands—don't even think it.

If there's something you believe in, have the decency
to keep it to yourself—no revelations, no irate
manifestos on the earth or deconstructions of the bed,
no uppercase god. There should be no nuns,
no old Baptist hymns in your poetry.

Employ
everything you need to make it happen,
that momentary stay against confusion, but include
no catalogs, no dogs.

The Mystery

> How great is the mystery that looks out of the eyes of a dog.
> —Margaret Washburn, *The Animal Mind*, 1912

Grown as old in her own years now
as anyone in town, Cleopatra,
deaf and blind, lies quietly all day

on the cool front stoop, flaps her tail,
smelling roast beef lowered to her bowl—
a lean, tender cut. The only sinners

in the universe, the only true dreamers
of eternity or even
another day, the only great explainers

can't explain, absolutely,
why a man might cry for his dog
harder than he did for his father;

though the man nearly knows
as he opens that hole in the back yard,
works to make it deep, breathing in

the sweetness of the earth.

Philosophy, with Illustrations

The paperback history of thought
cost fifteen cents. I discovered it
in a box of old books at a junk store, where
it belonged now, ruined by a child

with crayons, who had reddened Heraclitus, and who,
as if choosing to ignore or revere
every word set down in between,
had brightened up Schopenhauer, bearing down hard

with an orange and a green. Standing there
waiting on the book's once blank last page
is a figure with its arms set to fly;
with a body like a one-lane road;

with fingers like the petals of a sunflower, head
ballooned, hair floating just above
like a cloudy idea or a cloud;
with hollow round eyes drawn large; with perhaps

a smile, though it's easily a grimace,
on its one thick deep blue lip.

Comedian

When I sang those lines about Christ, who arose,
so the author of the hymn would have had it,
with a "triumph o'er his foes," I was four years old,
and proclaimed he had triumphed "o'er his clothes."

This provokes no more than a smile now,
as everything resides in the timing and the voice,
the occasion of surprise, but when my parents,
sitting at the kitchen table, heard my mistake,
they twisted and they bent like pines in the wind;
they howled and they coughed, until they both
crossed over into grief,
then grabbed me up and hugged me while I struggled,
angry and confused.
                        One afternoon,
working in the basement—I can't remember why,
but everyone was down there watching—my father
hit his head on a pipe, and the dull hollow bonk
of his skull meeting steel,
and then that expression on his face—less of pain
than of disbelief—set us all off,
nearly dropped my mother to the floor. I recall
their sitting on the steps in the half-dark,
how she laid his head over on her shoulder.

In the last two years of his life, my father
discovered that he couldn't pray aloud. His voice
thickened and it broke,
so that finally he asked to be excused
if the preacher called his name, and so he failed
to negotiate grace when we gathered
with our families.
                                    I think about the day
I saw him at the newly closed grave of his brother—
the only one younger, whose protector he had been
as a child—now dead by his own hand.
He might have been mistaken from a distance
for a man overtaken by a joke,
from the rhythm of his shoulders. When he laughed,
my father nearly barked his delight, gave a sharp
exhalation of surprise.
                                    I heard it happen
on the telephone the last time we talked. And if I
could sing with a child's wrong praise, even now,
I'd become that comedian of innocence again
gladly—to be gathered in their arms, baffled
by the sorrow that is not what it seems;
to be hurt once more by the laughter.

Two Poems for My Father

1. THE PRIZE

He still gets mail. Eight years in the grave,
he's achieved a kind of postal immortality.
A store keeps sending him its catalog; it wants
to know if he is ready for the winter. He receives
cruise information—you deserve to get away,
the letter will suggest. Unaware
how accurate they are, others write
telling him in large block letters
he's been chosen as a finalist. Yes,
he's now among the few who have qualified. In fact,
he may have won already, they will say, and he has,
he has. And how he gloried in the prize
they're offering: the chance of a lifetime.

2. APRIL 9

Today, my father's ten years old in heaven,
and he doesn't yet know what it is, this place
where the plate is a washed-out spot in the dirt,
first is a feed sack, second base and third,
wood scraps. Here,
there's a chicken wire fence, then a dirt road.
And on the other side of that, in the afternoons,
the women like to sit, shelling butter beans.
The sky here still turns red beyond the pines,
and when the breeze brings a single smell—
call it what you will—

of blossom, weeds, the broken earth, the rain;
when the crickets in the tall grass quit, all at once,
so the afternoon stalls where it is;
when his mother's shout rises from the house,
like nothing in a dream, and calls him home,
he is so filled then
with old, sad delight that day is done,
he knows, but then forgets, where he has gone.

Peace on Earth

Women's Correctional Institute, Hardwick, Georgia

The house close by goes dark after Christmas,
but the prison keeps lit year round; looped wire
shines like tinsel in a nightmare.

Inside, when they've written what I asked for,
some memory that's vivid with detail,
I am not quite ready.
                    If I think about Eve,
think of evil introduced into the world,
I remember how the snake liked to talk,
and I talk a little more.
                    Every night,
when I leave this place, I'm a free man, held
by the histories of women.
                    When the roads
open as they've never done before,
the women tell their stories in my head:
so many jagged scars for loving men;
                    God,
so many still pinned between Daddy and the bed.

Uneasy in my body, I have heard
a sentence fall apart, a woman's voice
choking on the thanks for what is hers,

for peace at last, for locks on all the doors.

Halloween at the Nursing Home

Every year, first day of October, there they are:
the sudden undead in the hallways;
the cartoon tombstones; too many skeletons
                              ready to dance;
and all those crones on brooms whose eyes gleam
and threaten, as though
they had flown in only to discover
they can never leave.
                    In time,
Thanksgiving will come,

but all October, the little ghosts,
one for each blade of the dining hall fans,
spin above the tables. They whirl, they celebrate
like hand puppets set free of the body,

their skirts flaring out on the long
                    carnival ride of the afterlife.

As if giddy with forever, they sweep
above the uncovered heads of the old women,
who do not look up.

Writing

But prayer was not enough, after all, for my father.
His last two brothers died five weeks apart.
He couldn't get to sleep, had no appetite, sat
staring. Though he prayed,
he could find no peace until he tried
to write about his brothers, tell a story
for each one: Perry's long travail
with the steamfitters' union, which he worked for;
and Harvey—here the handwriting changes,
he bears down—Harvey loved his children.

I discovered those few sheets of paper
as I looked through my father's old Bible
on the morning of his funeral. The others
in the family had seen them long ago;
they had all known the story,
and they told me I had not, most probably,
because I am a writer,
and my father was embarrassed by his effort. Yet
who has seen him as I can: risen

in the middle of the night, bending over
the paper, working close
to the heart of all greatness, he is so lost.

In Memory of Adrienne Bond

A great poem does not end. It will go on
inside the lucky ones who've heard it well,
who've caught its praise. And Adrienne was one.

A poem lays down the haze of winter dawn
to make us know some story we must tell
until we tell it right. It still goes on,

that spell against the night, that quiet song
made well, to hold the sad, the beautiful.
Few sing like that, but Adrienne was one.

There is no music deep enough to mourn
this woman whom we loved, no words to fill
our empty page but hers. And they go on

and say our names and tell us what we've known:
she moved within our lives as no one will.
This April day when Adrienne is gone,

something's broken in us all,
and that same thing is singing in us still.
A great poem does not end. It will go on.
It does go on. And Adrienne is one.

Homage

Let us now praise famous men, and our fathers.

—Ecclesiasticus 44:1

Our family in the 1930s was not
far different, if at all, from the Ricketts or the Gudgers.
In the old photographs, I have seen
the same angry squint, as if a boy
were shaken, unbelieving, from oblivion,
only minutes after coming from the cotton field—
his backbone throbbing like a bad tooth—
to return, hauling buckets of molasses
with arsenic to spread against the army worms,
the egg-laying flies and the boll weevil.

> Still,

it is not that connection I would make.
I think of James Agee and his gift. Even though,
in the sawmarked grain
of the sharecroppers' bare pine walls, he discovered—
swirling in the reds and peasant golds—
a poetry of agate and of silk, in the end,
he'd have chosen no words,
would have lifted up slivers of wood, bits of cloth,
musty lumps of earth to tell the story.

> And for me,

since a morning last April,
Agee puts it well: "a piece of body torn out
by the roots" would be truer than my words. But tonight,
only with my words,

I am holding up a King James Bible, inscribed
in 1942 by my mother,
and carried through the war, then forty more years—
the waxy black pebble-grain skin rubbed gray,
with patches like chamois to the hands, every page
ragged and frayed, and the gospels freed
from the spine.
             I am raising this Bible,
which is lying at his right hand, still, to let it praise
anyone, famous man or humble, whom it will.

Boys Playing Ball after Dark

IN MEMORY OF RAYMOND ANDREWS

A man takes a walk one afternoon
when the red sun's guttering in the pines,

and he doesn't wear a coat, though it's cold.
There's no one on the road. He will recall

the sweetness in the air, the burning leaves,
but this is what he loves:

discovering the boys playing ball
out of season, for as long as it is possible,

and the game going on after that,
so the boy at bat sees the silhouette

of the other child moving on the sky,
but not the ball, thrown and on its way.

He doesn't stop and interrupt their game
but still can hear their voices back at home,

and so he gives them names, he lets them talk,
he offers them a world, as from the dark,

he returns once again to his work.

The Funerals of Strangers

The funerals of strangers make us late,
delay us on the road, slow us down.

When the cars ease by, lights on, we will wait
patiently at first, but if the whole town

turns out, showing how it mourns, we can get
vexed at the dead, whose passing overflowed

the church close by, whose burial will set
a record for its holding of the road.

We do see clearly who we are, sitting there:
we're not the one followed to the graveyard.

And so, though we raise our arms in despair,
grimace, grip the steering wheel hard,

a quick thrill flickers in us all, looking on,
as it did inside that stranger, who is gone.

Together

When my father died,
I wanted everything to stop as he passed by,
the faces of the whole world turning like a field
of sunflowers.

And when a car backfires on the highway now,
every starling in the graveyard hovers near the earth,
then the flock swerves off like a black veil
swirling in the wind.

We stood there looking at the grave,
and my tears didn't come, this time,
until I turned to my mother,
and I saw hers.

We are sitting on a cold stone bench,
and when the flock startles upward with the noise,
my mother's hand tightens on mine, and she says
"Goodness," nothing else.

Goodness indeed, I am thinking. The birds
turn together in the air above the dead.

The Drifting Blue

At the table near mine in the airport bar
they're whispering in a tongue I cannot name,
and still, I have to listen. Maybe she

is asking, *Will you miss me?* He could say,
for all I'll ever know, *You are the dream
that filled me as a child, that meant the world*

would open like a blossom. Then their time
is nearly gone, they've almost said goodbye,
their whispers turning rough. *And I will bring*

the drifting blue itself, I hear her promising,
I hear it when she's gone, *and I will bring
the light along the edge of everything.*

Click

A poem comes right with a click, like a box.

—Yeats

There's the box-and-one, too:
a two-two zone with the free man badgering the hotshot,
denying him the ball. Every day,

the shooter's in the gym,
where he makes these demands of himself: half an hour
of full-court sprints, alternating with foul shots;

fifty ten-footers off the board, right and left,
off the dribble; fifty jumpers from the top of the key,
fifty each from the corners and the wings. Most often,

he's alone, and he takes it all in:
how a single dark board splits the lane,
how the empty gym booms with the ball, how it echoes

with the squeaking of his shoes. This is not
optional, the pause just to gaze across the court
when the hardwood shines like the calm, deep heart

of McElroy's Pond. This is necessary, too,
for the Friday night game in a bandbox gym
on the Tennessee border, the crowd so shrill,

the teams keep playing long after the whistle.
In the last three minutes, every score
or close call sets off noise like a saw hitting metal.

It is all so simple, just then.
A single point down, only one breath left on the clock,
he slides by a pick at the top of the key,

and is out of himself,
is fingertips, wrist, elbow, and eyes.
When the shot clicks softly on the bottom of the net,

he can hear it.

Some Words for Bill Matthews

Those cold eyes aimed our way made it clear
we had laughed too hard. You proposed
words for the look that she had given us:
mirth control, you called it.

                    And today,
when I thought of that quip once again,
remembering how *silly*, in an early sense, meant
blessed in the spirit, I had gone out
shopping for a used car.

                    Everywhere I went,
they were calling old heaps *preowned*,
as though a service had been done:
they had preworn brake pads down, prebent
the fender, prereplaced the alternator,
they'd prerebuilt the clutch.

                    So each of us
is used; we're all vehicular: the word
takes us for a spin.
It honks the horn, violates the laws, gets us lost,
and trades us in.

                    The motor of the old new car
gave a low smoker's laugh
as I drove it off the lot this afternoon.
The jazzy bad news buzzed the radio. The road
moaned its only tune.

The Question

Wave of sorrow,
Do not drown me now.
—Langston Hughes

I

It stank like ripe fish, milk gone bad—
that store on Polk Road owned by Jackie Neal,
who saw it as a nation set apart,
a country where he got to make the laws: King Jackie,
ruler of the aisles; highest court
over every word spoken, over mops fallen still;
the keeper of the key to the toilet, absolute
owner of the tips. When he kicked me
with his steel-toed boots one morning, he explained
he didn't need a reason. He would spew
philosophies of race all day:
they looked like apes; holy scripture had decreed
their servitude forever; all they wanted
was to lie around in bed eating pigs' feet;
they bred like dogs; if you put them in the jungle,
they'd be swinging on vines, talking gibberish,
and wearing no clothes, and it wouldn't take a week.
What's more, Jackie said, they'd be happy there,
where they came from. I should have set him straight,
so this would be a story with at least
a trace of heroism, but it's not. I had heard
words like Jackie's all my life. I believed
people wouldn't change, and other things
occupied me then: Carla Middlebrooks
and the ride we would take each night, cruising out
in her father's old rattletrap Ford,

getting lost on purpose, every back road new,
the weed fields sweet, moon floating on the lake,
crickets in the grass, tires rasping underneath.
Nothing else mattered, not the store's rotting air,
not Jackie's unremarkable soliloquies. The one
black man working at the store—he was called
Chickenbone; I never knew his real name—
had endured Jackie's talk for half his life,
at sixty years of age still a bag boy, a boy
with grandchildren. Chickenbone and I, that day,
leaned back lazily, our crossed feet propped
on the stock—he had bought us both candy,
put his money on the register because
no one had a key—and then he told me,
chuckling just a bit at the white boy, what
was obvious, he said, but I'd never even guessed:
Jackie sold sugar to the bootleggers.
There's a damaged half grin that can stay
on the face of a man knocked stupid.
It was something like that, only different, the way
we gazed across the cans at one another,
having both only heard it at the store. We were not
glad, yet not quite sad. Satisfied
might say it—how we felt, kicked back like that,
knowing they had hauled Jackie Neal's shackled body
from the bottom of a creek in Franklin County.

2

In a well-known photograph, a black man's chained
to a bed frame. Assembled with the body
are the people who have lynched him. And it's clear
the photographer has tried to get the crowd in,
since the dead man's far to the left, relegated
to the scene's dim periphery, as if
he were almost irrelevant. Against
a boredom so thick it made me slow, I created
a perverse entertainment,
and now, nearly thirty years later,
it reminds me of the boys I have read about
who crawled for adventure near a fence
to sneak a look at Auschwitz:
I convinced two friends, and we drove out together
to a meeting being held in a cow pasture.
My parents had forbidden me to go,
shouted that I knew it wasn't right. Yes, I did,
but my argument was this: I'd rise above it;
I would study them with clinical detachment,
those idiots in sheets and pointed hats.
My parents didn't buy it, made me promise.
I promised them. I said the words and went.
When I look at that photograph now, it is not
the mutilated man I return to—
who appears strangely free—but the crowd
posing for eternity and squeezing in tight,
smiling for the camera. A head leans in
at the picture's edge, not to be denied
its rightful place. The gathering was this:
a long worship service, with the choir
in slightly different robes. I won't forget
the beauty of the cross. I often think

of standing there quietly; and how, out of habit,
when the leader of the group raised his hand
and commanded everyone to bow his head,
without a thought, at first, that's what I did.

3

I'm watching television with my son—blacks and whites
holding yet another forum
on the question. I don't tell him, but I think,
as I hear what fills those voices, there are things,
ordinary things, that can never be redeemed.
Frances Sheats worked thirteen years for my mother,
made a dollar every day. I can see her
standing at the stove, cooking turnip greens,
feigning anger as she runs me from the kitchen;
Frances, who would have no children of her own;
whom I came across once crying hard in the pantry,
and who looked me in the eyes but wouldn't answer.
She is gone now; history has taken her from where
she never should have been—in our rocking chair,
the old hymns mellow in her throat,
her low hum lulling me to sleep. She is lost
from all I'm free to love. One afternoon,
at a movie matinee, painted Africans
throwing spears chased a hero with a gun
across a rope bridge strung above a river.
An older boy behind me started shouting
to the white man—cut away the ropes, he advised:
if the blacks tumbled in, they would die,
as everybody knew they couldn't swim. Back at home,
when I asked her to explain what I had heard,

Frances shook her head, then pulled me to her lap
and held me like she did when I was tired.
The panel on the show grows loud at the end.
My son and I discuss what they have said,
and he walks to his room, then fires up his amp
and plays the hard, wailing riffs he has inherited
from unnamed men with their second-hand guitars,
who are still there, sitting on the back steps, long
after dark, after coming home burdened with the fields,
the factories, the kitchens, or the streets—no words
equal to their histories of loss, or at least
nothing you will ever hear from me.

The Foolishness of God Is Wiser Than Men

1 Corinthians 1:25

God's editors erased what they thought not right:
the lighter side of Christ, how Jesus laughed,
delighted, pierced with irony, surprised.

A child's first word could have done it;
or the feel of water firm beneath his feet;
or Pilate's simple question "What is truth?"

I believe he caught his sandal on a root;
that he shook his head, chuckling at himself,
humbled, but renewed; that it was men

who could not quite handle what it meant: Christ,
blessed by a great joke, going to his knees,
saying "mercy," saying "please."

Elegy for a Young Poet

> Better to be
> The tree
> Than the ants
> Working on this blue day.
> —from "Sunday," by Bill Richard Jr.

You knew this, Bill: all elegy will fail,
every word turn to air; that we are all

like autumn leaves, unconscious in the sun.
We turn, shine, dazzle, whisper, fall.

You knew this too: how the days
and the seasons that can never come again

must come again. The trees,
the rest of us, have work that must be done.

And one long blue day glory comes down
like the light in old photographs, son.

A World Beneath

We set about the task, dragged the mattock
and the post hole digger from the shed.
We divined the right spot beneath the oak.
I swung the pick six or seven times,

and the tool pulled me downward in its wake.
Resting in the shade, I came to think
if we didn't work faster,
we wouldn't get to China until well past dark.

But I wondered who would pull us up again
from the country that was always underneath,
where the people might have never even heard
they were living in a miracle—

a world beneath another;
how they dangled upside down but did not fall.

2

I dropped to the ground, unlaced heavy high-tops,
peeled off grimy white socks,
and stepped onto cool cut grass
as the pines and the live oaks blackened, the brick

of the small house giving up the buttery glow
only sundown brought. It was time
to run alone over that chilled green shadow
where the yard sloped down toward the chicken wire,

and to ask, not calling up the syllables, but
in the language of blue jeans flapping at my ankles,
if anyone could run that fast.
And there came no answer, only this:

the chuckle of my father's Chevrolet,
rolling down the long gravel driveway.

3

On a bright late August afternoon, Uncle Johnny
lit a thin panetella, and the rich, bitter smell
mingled with the odor of manure, carried
on a hot breeze cutting through a hog farm

to linger in my grandmother's yard. They had laid
the long two-by-eights across saw horses
and loaded those makeshift tables
with roast beef, barbeque, skillet-fried chicken,

collard greens, field peas, tart pickled peaches,
gallon jars of iced tea sweeter than the pies.
And when the heat waves liquified the air
near the barn's tin roof,

the men lay beached on the screened front porch,
many with the same long nose, same chin,
but they all showed the heaviness; their eyes
tried to close.

4

There is only one story of hunting I can tell.
At twelve, I would drift in the far back pasture
of my grandfather's dairy farm,
firing at pine stumps, limbs, tin cans

balanced on outcroppings. Often I would load
the single-shot .22, draw a tight bead
on a buzzard in a slow arc brushing the clouds,
try to gauge how far I should lead him,

then carefully squeeze. Never once
did I ruffle a feather,
so I turned back finally to things close by.
I could say I didn't really want to kill,

but to move one finger and to change
the heavens, yet in truth,
what I wanted was to watch a body fall that far,
and to hear it hit the earth.

5

When the small white flowers of the blackberry flare
then quickly disappear,
the cool dusk air fills with honeysuckle,
and a smell still comes from the cotton fields:

like a cross-breeze washing through a cellar,
a faint ammonia cut with musty weed
that can sting the eyes bright. Driving home
on the blacktop Sunday afternoon,

when my daughter's face twisted with her question,
I inhaled the insecticide deeply, drew it in
till it touched every summer of my life; I explained
it was poison, though I drove on slowly, and as if

I could never get enough.

Prayer

Who is equal to a seed, piece of wood, plain rock,
or any simple thing? Whose words are enough
for the ocher leaf floating to the earth

on the journey of its life? Who can rise
to its falling; who will feel it on his tongue,
the oak's new foliage of sky? So if we

should find no words in a graveyard, where's
the bulletin in this? Let us practice,
in unison, our lullaby of silence.

Let us offer each glance, every step
we take among the graves as a paying of respects,
but in ways we can't conceive. And if the past

should gather like a storm, loom ahead;
and if the future should return
as a room closed off now, windowless and still,

let us lift a bit of dust or blade of grass
and release it here, an offering to the air,
a brief, mute prayer for the breeze—easy lover

of the skin, lonely mother of the breath.

Calvin's Wife

In Puritan belief, each shuffle of the cards
or rolling of the dice was a sin.
But not because the players put their families at risk,
and not because gain came easily, or that
it happened most often in the alehouse, home
to Jezebels and drunks. What really mattered
was the window into providence. Because
the Lord set forth his plan in every breeze,
each petal as it fell, every filament of dust
twisting at the windowsill, *chance*
was a heathen word, offered by the lost.
So it followed: any showing of the deal,
all rolling of the soothsayer's bones,
was a trifling with design, a sleazy glance
at holiness. But there she is again
in the line at the Quickie Mart, buying one shot
at the Powerball. Tonight,
when she walks outside with her ticket,
a haze of bugs swirls above the gas pumps, wild
with the light—every feint, flit, and swerve
invisibly determined. If she wins,
she'll quit her job, her hair will never smell
like the poultry plant again. She will invest,
let the money do the work, let someone else
check the chicken guts for spots, and yet the God-
given odds tell us this:
tomorrow, she'll be up before the sun,
put the ugly green uniform on, pop the hood
of Calvin's old Ford to get it started, as she does
every day. Chances are,
when the dying car coughs itself to life,

when she guides it from the yard and down the road,
where the wet streets gleam as if shined by hand,
where the windowpanes blaze blackened red,
where the paper trash scatters with the breeze,
she will let herself praise another day, made glad
as if God still numbered every hair
on her head.

Going Home

You have seen these women at the steering wheel,
an old man riding in the right front seat,
his heart unreliable, his eyes finding haze,

or maybe he is mapping out routes to a home
only in the past. All of us
have followed those old women going too slow

down two-lane roads. We have taken our place
in the long line of cars. And some of us,
released by a straightaway, raise one palm

in disbelief, the other hand steady on the horn.
We roar past, brandishing a face. Later on,
we'll come to understand she's not the problem,

which is always, somehow, time.
It's the sun too bright on the asphalt slick
with afternoon rain; it's the cloud brought low

in the field beside the road; the crackling hiss
of the tires racing past. And which of those
old women going home doesn't know this?

Laughter

1

If a line of cars following a hearse rolls past,
local custom still obtains: until it's gone,
every other car occupies the shoulder of the road.
But today, there's a hearse with a flat tire
by the highway, the undertaker's men working fast,
like a pit crew called out far too close
to the checkered flag. Lug nuts freeze,
so the funeral has stalled beside the road
and the protocol's reversed:
the ordinary traffic travels on; behind the hearse,
relatives and friends sit waiting to resume
the afternoon chore. They are not, all of them,
solemn in their grief—some laugh,
as if greatly entertained; we can see it. As for us,
perhaps we're amused now too, maybe we
are silly with a pain all our own, driving off
laughing as if cracked along the funny bone.

2

The man next door makes the world news. First,
little girls all over town, including yours,
begin to disappear. The authorities will find,
much later, he has lured them to his house,
and what he's done then,
no one must imagine, since the news tells it all.
He cuts them up and puts them into food
he delivers each time (this does him in)

to the folks whose child he has violated. Say
you recall what the casserole tasted like,
the bites he made you eat against your appetite,
insisting he had gone to so much trouble;
how he said he'd made it special, just for you.
And when everyone's familiar with the news,
in break rooms, schoolyards, offices, and bars,
the jokes will metastasize, laughter will arise.
This will happen not too far from where you are.

The Widow's Desire

1

If some things happen for a reason, she believes,
others simply are.

As she looks on, sitting by herself
near the back one bleak Sunday morning;
as the gospel choir starts on the chorus

following a long, slow verse; as the man,
with one quick sweep of his arm, sets the choir
swaying to a picked-up rhythm, this is what

gives her such a chill, this coincidence:

as the man whips the group into step,
as the bright new unison begins, just then,
the sun comes streaming through the windows,

as if the song brought a change in the weather
or the heavens had rehearsed with the choir.

2

She finds herself following a baseball team
on the TV. Secretly, she talks
to the players and the manager. She knows

the nicknames. She always checks the paper
for the average of her favorite, the catcher,
in the slump of his career. She develops

an opinion on artificial turf, as her boys
lose too often on the rug, and it's ugly.
Her own arms ache

when they talk about the cortisone shots
for the shortstop's elbow. Now,
on a clear, perfect evening in June,

she goes to bed saddened by the rain.

3

Mary Ann Laney's lost her job, and there she is,
raising those children all alone.
Willie Connor's got cancer. Carl Sims, an old friend,

has some trouble with the law. All assembled
in the basement of the church hear the names,
and they pray for each one. Then at home,

when she turns off the late world news,
those faces on the screen keep crying—
people she will never see again, whose grief

she has just clicked off.
The telephone rings. There is no one on the line.
Another ring. No one. When it rings

again, she could slap God hard, the way she would
any man she loved
who remained where he was, watching anything at all,

without a word.

4

Talking on the phone to her sister, she begins
looking at the moths on the windowpane,
the brown wavy marks on their papery wings
like layers of water stain. Static on the line

interrupts, and they talk about the static,
then the prices at the market downtown,
the bargains this week. When she hangs up,
she thinks about standing in a barn, long ago,

waiting out a thunderstorm; how,
when the rain slacked off, she and Wilson
had kept on standing in the door. Her desire
is to breathe that air once more,

cattle smells and wet pine rising on a breeze
sweetened by the rain, to claim the air
washing in cool through a cornfield,
across the oily hot motor of the John Deere.

5

She dreams there is someone in the house, dreams
she goes down into the basement,
clatters through the tools till she finds it,

and eases up the steps with a hammer. Halfway,
it grows too heavy for her arms.
But someone's in the house,

and the sound now comes from the basement.
She opens up a door off the stairwell, a door
she has never even seen. And underneath

her own small house, she discovers
another one—a large, warm home. Somehow,
a family has gathered, and a silly little boy

makes everybody laugh, and she stands there
quietly at the door, wondering who they are.

The Multitude

The woman in the airplane wanted
to talk about Christ. I did not.
I raised my magazine. She continued, saying Christ
promised heaven to the thief
who believed while nailed to the cross.
The clouds looked solid far beneath. She began
the story of her life, and I stopped her
as politely as I could, saying please, right now,
I'd simply like to read. And for a while,
she did keep quiet, then she asked
if I'd ever really given Christ a chance, so I tried
telling her a joke, chose the one
about the Pope and Richard Nixon in a rowboat.
She discovered nothing funny in the story.
Jesus fed the multitude, she said.
I looked around to find an empty seat.
There wasn't one. She asked me if I knew
about the sower and the seed; about Zaccheus;
Legion and the swine; Mary Magdalene;
Lazarus; the rich young ruler. And I did,
I knew about them all. I told her yes,
sweet Jesus; got the stewardess
to bring another a bourbon; tried to buy
the missionary one, but she declined.
And when the plane set down,
I'd escaped up the aisle, made the door,
and started walking fast toward the baggage claim,
when I saw them, all at once, on the concourse:
thousands I would never see again, who'd remain

nothing in my life, who would never have names;
and I realized I'd entertained—strangely,
and for no good reason I could see—
the hope of someone waiting there
who loved me.

Home

The stroke-addled old folks drooling all day;
the women holding baby dolls, calling them by name;
the swollen-tongued toothless in their wheelchairs;

the wrinkled infants sitting in their own fresh waste;
the mange-haired talkers with their questions;
the skeletons with clothes on, skulls wearing skin

like tissue paper pasted on the bone—on and on,
the wailing wall-eyed horror that they were
when I first appeared among them with my mother.

Then a history of groans began to grow,
till the sing-song noise made sense; till the wild
rocking side to side said welcome; till the mouth

locked forever in its O spoke of home.

Surrender

We were ordinary men,
unable to embrace each other fully—
to bury a face in the other man's neck,
to rock like drunks in the doorway, saying
goodbye. It was always a handshake
and maybe that sideways hug,
with an arm around the shoulders.
                                    In the hospital
you couldn't understand, didn't know me,
tried to overturn the rack by the bed, tear
the needles from your arm; searched everywhere,
underneath the sheets and the pillow,
for your clothes, "going home"; grew frightened
when confused by the purpose of a spoon, angry
when you couldn't even urinate—failing
to hit the plastic bottle, till I held you.
If I leaned down close
when the baffled agitation started up,
and I smoothed back your hair, or I kissed you
on the forehead or the cheek, whispered "Daddy,"
you'd throw your arms around me.

There's a way a man turns to a woman,
so his lips just barely graze hers, yet in this,
there is everything that follows, each detail
of forgetting where they are.
And today I am trembling with desire, wild
for the years, when my lips feel yours, cool
as gold. One kiss for the infinite
particulars of love, to tell you this:

I will be with you there, in the darkness.

A Postcard to My Father

Alone in a strange place now,
I often think of you,

and when the meeting broke early here in Jacksonville,
I walked back alone to my room,
made a drink, then relaxed on the balcony, the sea
indigo and palm-leaf green,
whitecaps far beyond the waves.

I lay across the bed, and then the dark
surprised me. I hadn't meant to sleep.

At dinner, people talked about the storm.
They had gathered at the windows of the bar
for the arteries of light branching out,
for the rain boiling silver on the asphalt,
for the palms bending low. You should have seen it,

they told me more than once,
you should have seen it.

In the Sweet By and By

I had seen the earth open and close, the golden ash
of pollen wash away, each thin copper spine
of broom sage bending in the dawn,

as if burdened by the shining of the sun;
I had stared at the dirt; tried to reason what it meant
if the moon flared white on a wet tin roof,

if the clover bowed waving in the wake of every car,
if the petals of the dogwoods fell;
I had sat drinking coffee in the all-night diner,

with one good question for the universe
if people still joked at the counter,
if the hot grill hissed like rain,

if the rain fell softly in the parking lot;
like a slow child puzzled by a story's end,
I had kicked up dust to watch it float;

I had stumbled out stunned some days, like a boy
still lost in the afternoon movie, unprepared
for the late sun burning in the street;

but when I stood with my mother in the church,
a month since we had left him in the earth;
when the years swirled back like weather, there,

where the windows thrown open in July, long ago,
brought creosote and pine smells, freshly cut grass,
let the trucks' low groans on the highway rise

with every old anthem, every prayer;
where revivals once built all week like desire,
so the quiet in the worship hall crackled,

bristling with a charge, as if fire might arc
between the Word and the not-yet-saved;
where the preacher lay an everlasting weight

on the one final stanza we would sing;
where he pleaded with the lost until the yawn
of eternity began with the hymn's last note;

where I stood with my mother in the back row now,
found the melody and followed it, as though
there were nothing else to do; and when I heard

the alto my mother used to sing
at the ironing board or working in her flower bed
or standing at the sink, each note told the truth:

though the days break new in a mockingbird's throat,
and a gauzy mist stalls above a creek bed, spins,
as if conscious of its body in the light;

though a dying man can't help laughing at a joke,
so he rocks in his own wasted arms;
and a rain cloud leans like a barn set to fall,

while the wind starts to whistle in the wires;
and though a woman lies back on the loading dock,
waiting for her ride while the sky turns red,

and a girl leaving work at the truck stop walks
toward a greasy strip of grass beyond the parking lot,
as the breeze cuts across the wisteria, its smell

mingled with the diesel and the smoke;
though the boys looking hard for a lost ball pause
for the brief wild sugar of the honeysuckle,

and a galaxy will whirl through the wilderness
like an oak leaf wheeling toward a roof; even though
the clover and the dogwoods bloom, we become

nothing, not the actors in a dream, not the mist,
not a new stone lowered into earth. We are like
the hymns once played on the out-of-tune piano

in the living room, harmonies defined
by the family that stood there—versions no one else
will ever reproduce. Sunday morning,

as we struggled through the chorus, there it was,
still, in my mother's soft alto—the old
promise in her voice.

An Introduction

You who break the dark all night, whisper and shout,
who travel in and out of all the rooms,
who come with pill or needle, vial or chart,
with bedding, mop and bucket, tray of food;
who turn, clean, pull, read, record, pat, and go;
who see her hair matted by the pillow, greasy white
wild short hair that will shock
anyone from home who hasn't seen her for a while—
shocking like her bones, showing now;
like the plum-colored bruises on her arms; like her face
when she first comes to and what it says; like her mouth
and the anything it says: *Call the dogs,* or
I've got to go to school, or *Tonight y'all roll
that wagon wheel all the way to Mexico;* you
who have seen three children—unbelieving, unresigned—
in all these rooms, full of anger and of prayer;
you who change her diaper, empty pans
of green and gold bile she has puked up; you
who cannot help breathing her decay,

I would like to introduce you to our mother,
who was beautiful, her eyes like nightshade,
her wavy brown hair with a trace of gold; Myrtle,
whose alto flowed through the smooth
baritone our father used to sing;
our mother, who would make us cut a switch,
but who rocked us and who held us and who kissed us;
Myrtle, wizard typist, sharp with figures,
masterful with roses and with roast beef;

who worked for the New Deal Seed Loan Program,
for the school, local paper, county agent, and the church;
who cared long years for her own failing mother
(whom she worries for now; you may have heard her);
who was tender to a fault, maybe gullible,
as the truly good and trusting often are; and even so,
who could move beyond fools, though foolishness itself
delighted her—a double-take, words turned around,
a silly dance—and when our mother laughed
(I tell you this because you haven't heard it),
the world could change, as though the sun could shine
inside our very bones.

                And where it's written in Isaiah
that the brier won't rise, but the myrtle tree,
there's a promise unfulfilled:
she will not go out with joy.
Still, if you had known her, you yourselves,
like Isaiah's hills, would sing. You'd understand
why it says that *all the trees
of the field shall clap their hands.*